CRIME SOLVERS

WITHDRAWN

DETERMINING

THE CAUSE OF DEATH

by Melissa Langley Biegert

Consultant:
David Foran, PhD
Director, Forensic Science Program
Michigan State University

Reading Consultant:
Barbara J. Fox
Reading Specialist
North Carolina State University

Capstone
press

Mankato, Minnesota

Blazers is published by Capstone Press,
151 Good Counsel Drive, P.O. Box 669, Mankato, Minnesota 56002.
www.capstonepress.com

Books published by Capstone Press are manufactured with paper
containing at least 10 percent post-consumer waste.

Library of Congress Cataloging-in-Publication Data
Biegert, Melissa Ann Langley, 1967–
    Determining the cause of death / by Melissa Langley Biegert.
    p. cm. — (Blazers. Crime solvers)
    Summary: "Describes methods used by experts to determine the cause of death to solve
crimes" — Provided by publisher.
    Includes bibliographical references and index.
    ISBN 978-1-4296-3375-8 (lib. bdg.)
    1. Forensic pathology — Juvenile literature. 2. Autopsy — Juvenile literature. 3. Criminal
investigation — Juvenile literature. I. Title. II. Series.
RA1063.4.B48 2010
614'.1 — dc22   2009014604

Editorial Credits
Megan Schoeneberger, editor; Matt Bruning, designer; Eric Gohl, media researcher

Photo Credits
Alamy/Zefa RF, 25
AP Images/Joe Cavaretta, 9
Capstone Press/Karon Dubke, badge (all), cover (all), 4, 5, 11, 12, 15, 16, 20 (both), 27, 28, 30
Corbis SABA/Shepard Sherbell, 21
Getty Images Inc./Stone/Joel Rogers, 7
iStockphoto/Eddie Green, 6
Newscom/KRT Photos/The Record/James W. Anness, 29; KRT Photos/San Jose Mercury News/
    Patrick Tehan, 22–23
Shutterstock/AVAVA, 18; ene, 26; Leah-Anne Thompson, 19; Loren Rodgers, 10

CRIME SOLVERS

DETERMINING THE CAUSE OF DEATH

TABLE OF CONTENTS

no. 073822901

CHAPTER ONE

DEATH AND MYSTERY

A man has died suddenly. Did he die naturally? Was it an accident? Or was it murder?

BLAZERS FACT

Heart disease causes the most sudden deaths in the United States.

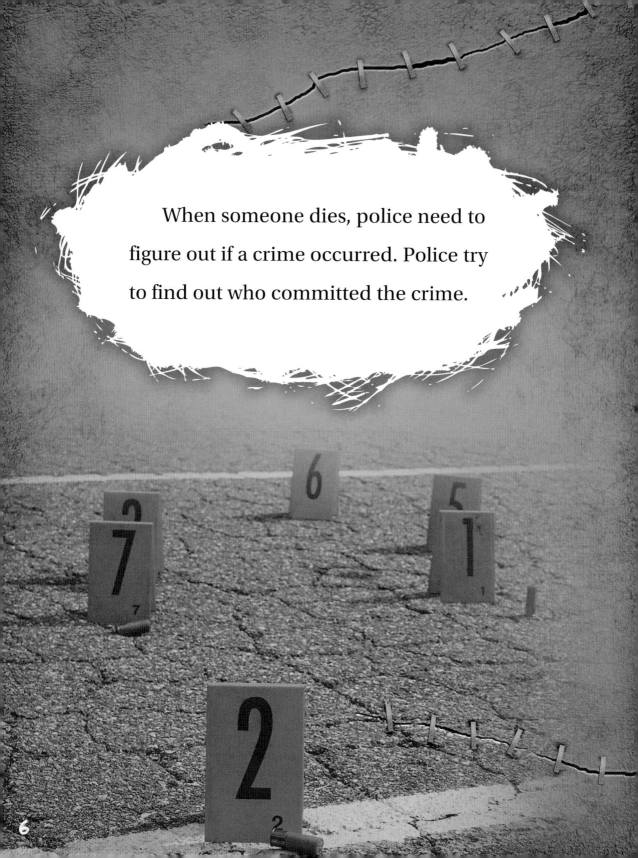

When someone dies, police need to figure out if a crime occurred. Police try to find out who committed the crime.

BLAZERS FACT

A murder occurs about once every 30 minutes in the United States.

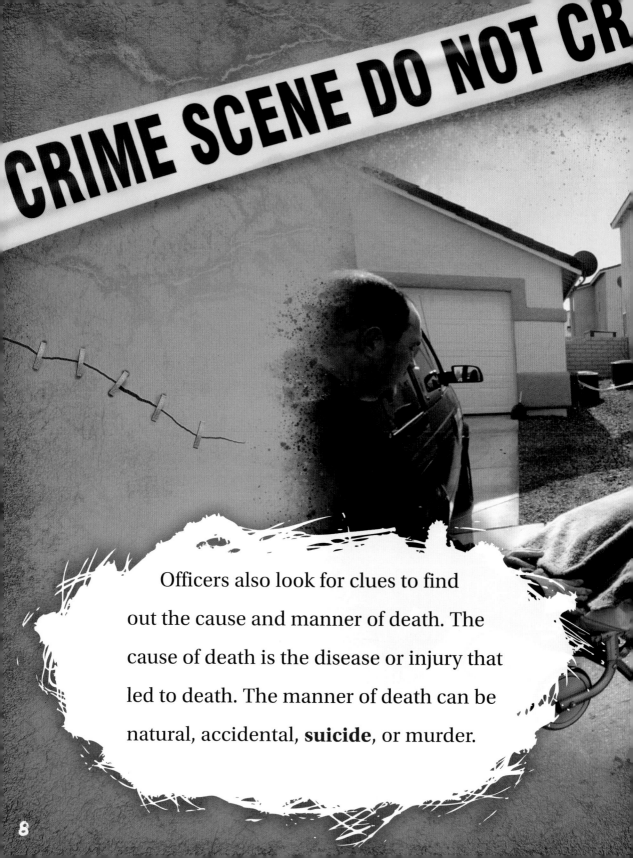

CRIME SCENE DO NOT CR

Officers also look for clues to find out the cause and manner of death. The cause of death is the disease or injury that led to death. The manner of death can be natural, accidental, **suicide**, or murder.

suicide – the taking of one's own life

CHAPTER TWO

ON THE SCENE

Police check the body and crime scene for clues. They take photographs. They also take blood samples to be tested. These clues will help show the cause and manner of death.

BLAZERS FACT

Police began using photography to record crime scenes as early as 1865.

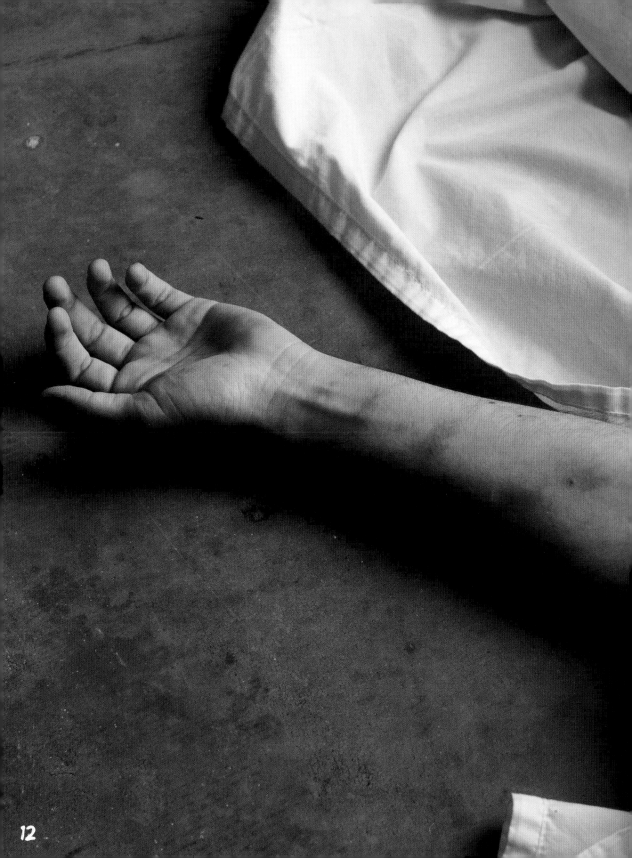

Police look for bruises on a body. Bruises occur when something hard hits the skin. They result from an attack or an accident.

BLAZERS FACT

Fresh bruises are usually dark blue or purple.

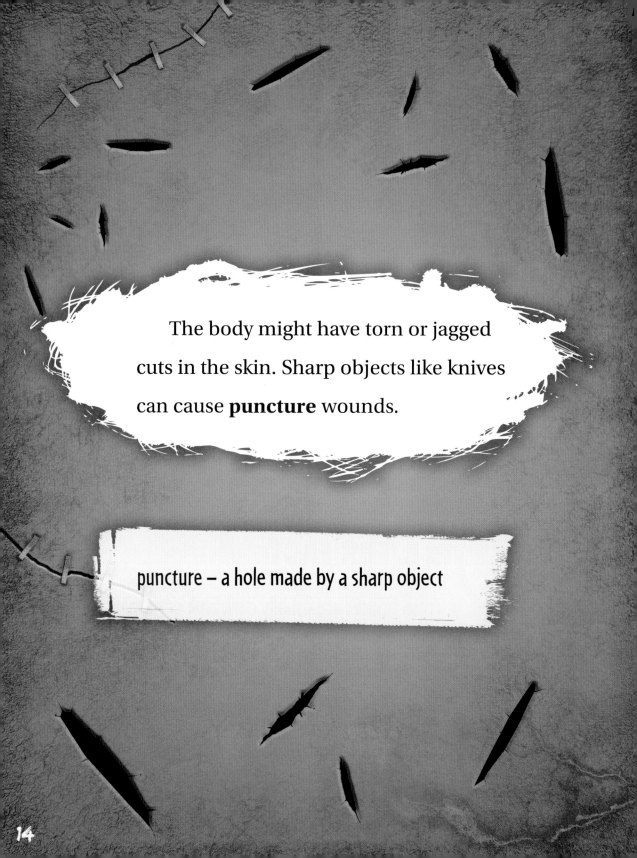

The body might have torn or jagged cuts in the skin. Sharp objects like knives can cause **puncture** wounds.

puncture – a hole made by a sharp object

14

Police also look for **defensive** wounds. These injuries happen when victims try to protect themselves during an attack. Defensive wounds are usually on the arms or hands.

defensive – intended to protect

CHAPTER THREE

IN THE LAB

After police collect **evidence**, the body is taken to the **medical examiner** (ME). This doctor closely examines the body. The ME determines the official cause and manner of death.

evidence – information, items, and facts that help prove something to be true or false

medical examiner – a specially trained doctor who rules on official causes and manners of deaths

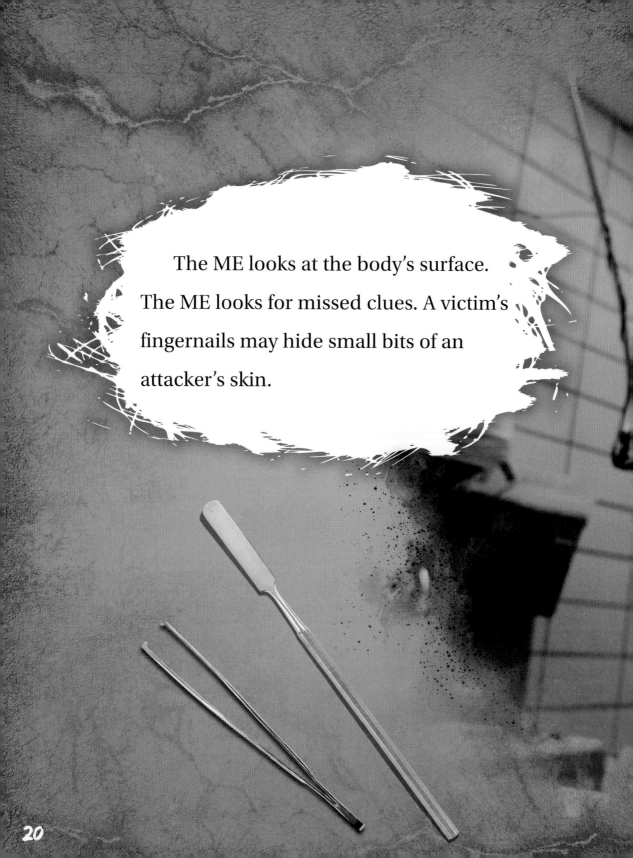

The ME looks at the body's surface. The ME looks for missed clues. A victim's fingernails may hide small bits of an attacker's skin.

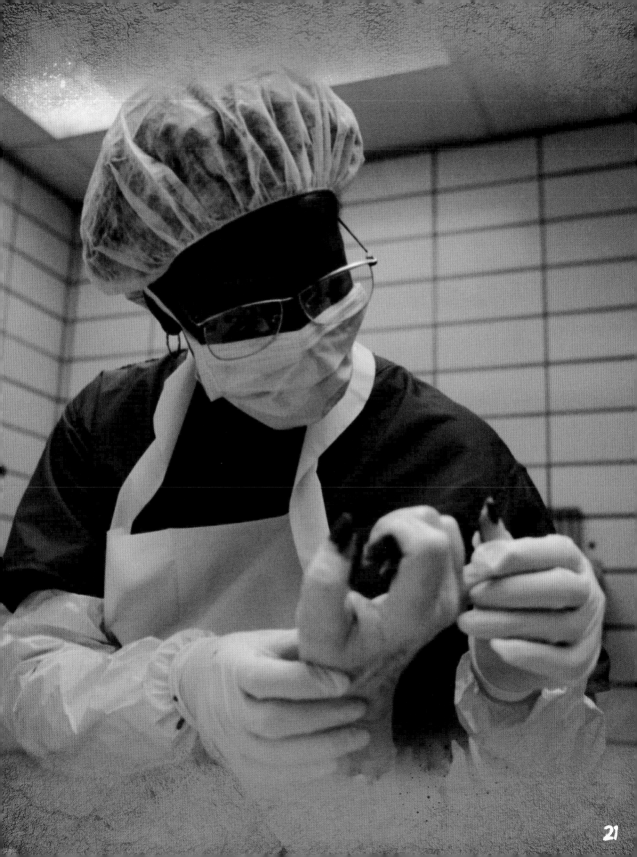

Next, the ME takes x-rays and other images of the body. These pictures show broken bones, foreign objects, or **internal** injuries.

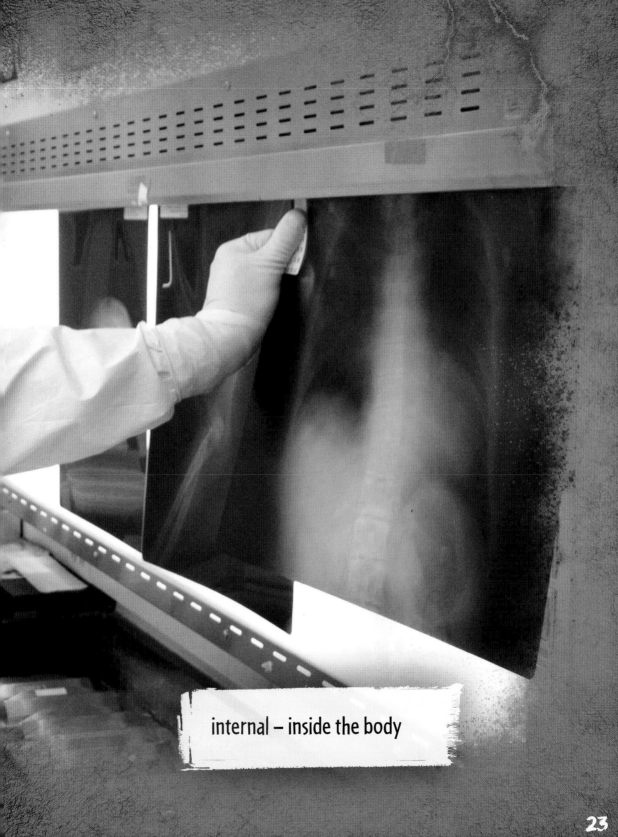

internal – inside the body

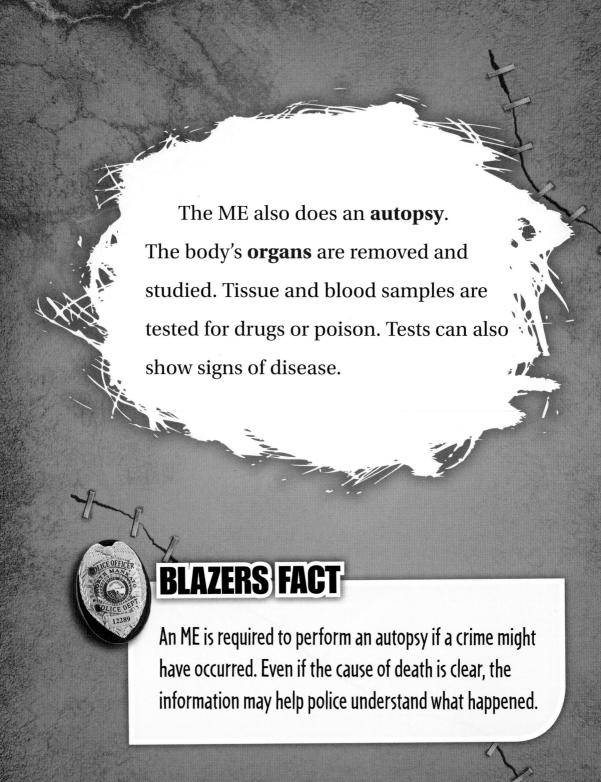

The ME also does an **autopsy**. The body's **organs** are removed and studied. Tissue and blood samples are tested for drugs or poison. Tests can also show signs of disease.

BLAZERS FACT

An ME is required to perform an autopsy if a crime might have occurred. Even if the cause of death is clear, the information may help police understand what happened.

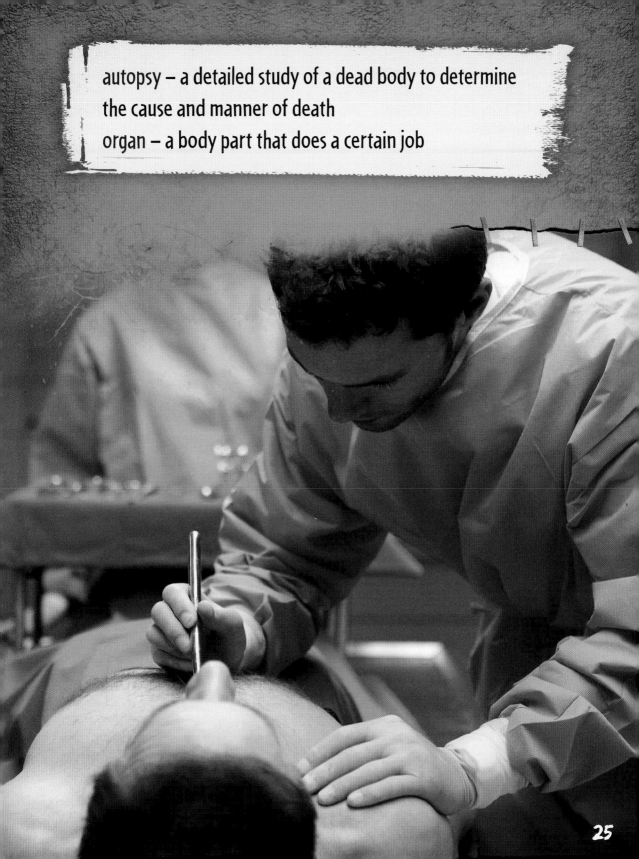

autopsy – a detailed study of a dead body to determine the cause and manner of death

organ – a body part that does a certain job

CHAPTER FOUR

CAUSES AND CHARGES

The ME goes over evidence from the tests. The ME then gives the official cause and manner of death. In some rare cases, doctors never find the cause of death.

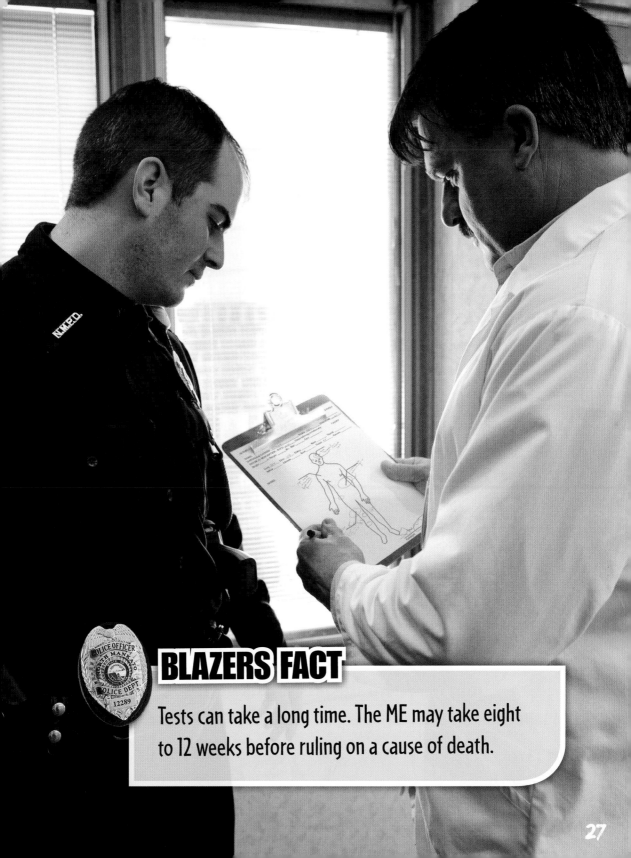

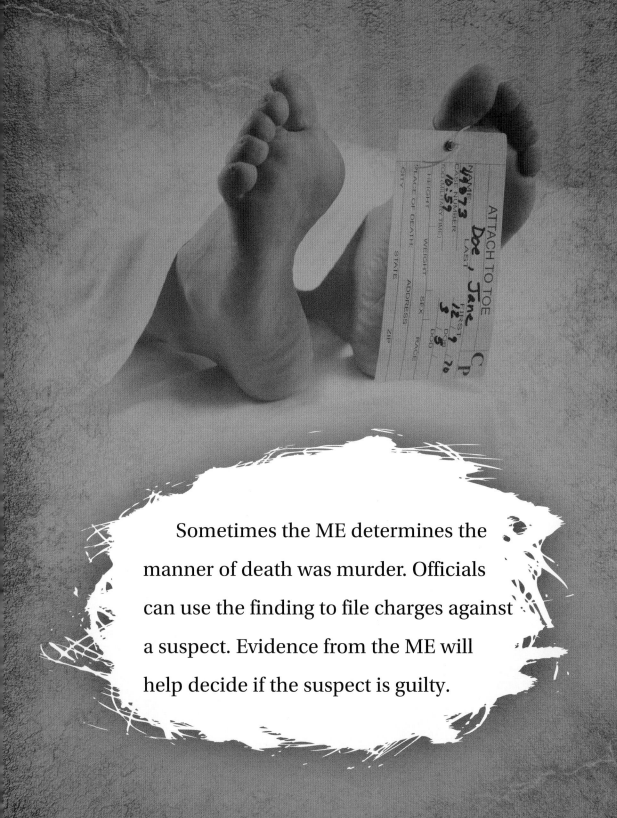

Sometimes the ME determines the manner of death was murder. Officials can use the finding to file charges against a suspect. Evidence from the ME will help decide if the suspect is guilty.

New tests have led some MEs to change their rulings years after the deaths.

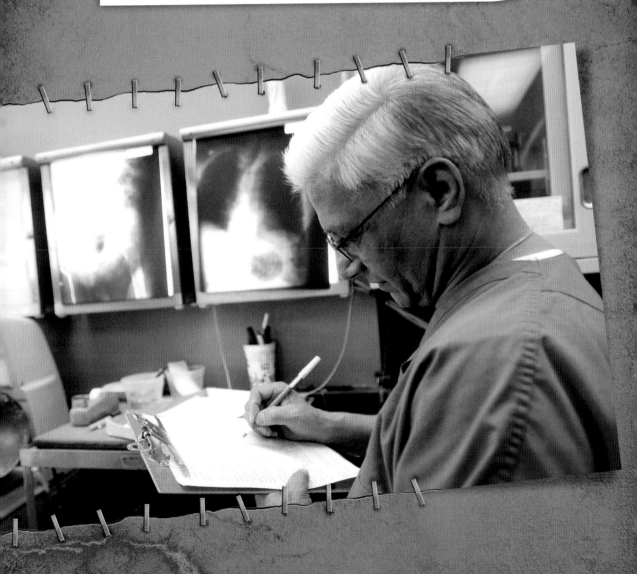

Glossary

autopsy (AW-top-see) — a detailed study of a dead body to determine the cause and manner of death

defensive (di-FEN-siv) — intended to protect

evidence (EV-uh-duhnss) — information, items, and facts that help prove something to be true or false

internal (in-TUR-nuhl) — inside the body

medical examiner (MED-uh-kuhl eg-ZAM-in-ur) — a specially trained doctor who rules on official causes and manners of deaths

organ (OR-guhn) — a body part that does a certain job

puncture (PUHNGK-chur) — a hole made by a sharp object

suicide (SOO-uh-side) — the taking of one's own life

tissue (TISH-yoo) — a layer or bunch of soft material that makes up body parts

Read More

Ballard, Carol. *At the Crime Scene!: Collecting Clues and Evidence.* Solve That Crime! Berkeley Heights, N.J.: Enslow, 2009.

Beck, Esther. *Cool Forensic Tools: Technology at Work.* Cool CSI. Edina, Minn.: ABDO, 2009.

Sitford, Mikaela. *Serial Killer File: The Doctor of Death Investigation.* Crime Solvers. New York: Bearport, 2008.

Internet Sites

FactHound offers a safe, fun way to find Internet sites related to this book. All of the sites on FactHound have been researched by our staff.

Here's all you do:

Visit *www.facthound.com*

FactHound will fetch the best sites for you!

Index